THE PHOENIX GONE,
THE TERRACE EMPTY

Also by Marilyn Chin

Revenge of the Mooncake Vixen
Rhapsody in Plain Yellow
Dwarf Bamboo

THE PHOENIX GONE
THE TERRACE EMPTY

poems

Marilyn Chin

milkweed
editions

© 2009, Text by Marilyn Chin
All rights reserved. Except for brief quotations in critical articles
or reviews, no part of this book may be reproduced in any manner
without prior written permission from the publisher: Milkweed
Editions, 1011 Washington Avenue South, Suite 300, Minneapolis,
Minnesota 55415.
(800) 520-6455
www.milkweed.org

Published 2009 by Milkweed Editions
Printed in the United States of America
Cover design by Jeenee Lee
Cover photo: Seeley Davidson
Author photo by Niki Berg
The text of this book is set in Calisto.
16 17 18 19 20 11 10 9 8 7
First Edition

Please turn to the back of this book for a list of the sustaining funders
of Milkweed Editions.

ISBN 978-1-57131-439-0

The Library of Congress has cataloged the previous edition as follows:

Chin, Marilyn.
    The Phoenix Gone, The Terrace Empty / by Marilyn Chin.—1st ed.
        p.   cm.
    ISBN 0-915943-87-5
    1. Asian American women—Poetry. 2. Asian Americans—Poetry.
    I. Title
    PS3553.H48975P48 1994
    811'.54—dc20
                                                    93-33206
                                                        CIP

CONTENTS

ACKNOWLEDGMENTS

I would like to thank the National Endowment for the Arts, the Wallace E. Stegner Fellowship at Stanford University, the Corporation of Yaddo, the MacDowell Colony, the Djerassi Foundation, and San Diego State University. I would like to thank my secretary and friend Martha Razo. This book would not have been possible without their generous support.

Journals:
The American Voice
Caliban
Five Fingers Review
The Iowa Review
The Kenyon Review
Parnassus
Ploughshares
Quarry West
Quarterly West
Seneca Review
Wooster Review
ZYZZYVA

Anthologies:
Looking for Home, edited by Deborah Keenan and Roseann
    Lloyd, Milkweed Editions, 1990
Ms. Twentieth Anniversary issue, Summer/Fall, 1992
The Open Boat, edited by Garrett Hongo, Anchor/Viking, 1992

On the publication of this fifteenth anniversary edition, I am grateful for the opportunity to thank some important folks. First of all, I thank Emilie Buchwald who chose *Phoenix* for publication. I thank the successive posses at Milkweed for their kind sustenance.

I thank the numerous scholars, editors, and teachers—too many to name—who worked hard to give my poems a place at the table. Thanks to them, the poems in *Phoenix* have been anthologized hundreds of times and have been taught all over the world in courses ranging from MFA craft workshops to Introduction to Literature classes; from Asian-American Literature to Women's Studies; from Literature of the Diaspora to Ethno Poetics. During my recent visit to Beijing, a scholar included my poems in a future course called Bilingual Poetics.

Again, and most of all, my dear readers, I want to thank you for your lively participation, for the love and passion that you've bestowed upon these poems for fifteen years. Thank you for keeping the beautiful she-bird singing.

PRELUDE

To love your country
is to know its beginnings
not with the bald-face moon
or the complacent river—
but here within you.

Your heart is a house—
I/we are its inhabitants.
Although the country is lost
rivers and mountains remain.
And we shall always live
in this poetry that you love.

for my mother,
Wong Yuet Kuen

THE PHOENIX GONE,
THE TERRACE EMPTY

EXILE'S LETTER

EXILE'S LETTER:
after the failed revolution

A world exists beyond the limits of this pane.
Truly, there are higher vistas, better gazebos,
miraculous avenues beyond these closed doors.
Not to mention a poet humbler and kinder than myself
somewhere between Cold Mountain and Lake Lopnor—
who may never write again, and for whom
the sun rises and sets only peripherally now
as she threshes wheat or forces silk from mulberries,
not hers, as she walks into exile vowing no return—
she looks up, finds my face in the moon.

"Dear Cousin, do not mourn me or this empty sky,
for the sky is limitless. Ah, yet, there is a limit
to even 'sky.' Like you we are fallow deer;
on Regret Road we must not tarry."

HOW I GOT THAT NAME

an essay on assimilation

I am Marilyn Mei Ling Chin.
Oh, how I love the resoluteness
of that first person singular
followed by that stalwart indicative
of "be," without the uncertain i-n-g
of "becoming." Of course,
the name had been changed
somewhere between Angel Island and the sea,
when my father the paperson
in the late 1950s
obsessed with a bombshell blonde
transliterated "Mei Ling" to "Marilyn."
And nobody dared question
his initial impulse—for we all know
lust drove men to greatness,
not goodness, not decency.
And there I was, a wayward pink baby,
named after some tragic white woman
swollen with gin and Nembutal.
My mother couldn't pronounce the "r."
She dubbed me "Numba one female offshoot"
for brevity: henceforth, she will live and die
in sublime ignorance, flanked
by loving children and the "kitchen deity."
While my father dithers,
a tomcat in Hong Kong trash—
a gambler, a petty thug,
who bought a chain of chopsuey joints
in Piss River, Oregon,
with bootlegged Gucci cash.
Nobody dared question his integrity given
his nice, devout daughters
and his bright, industrious sons

as if filial piety were the standard
by which all earthly men were measured.

.

Oh, how trustworthy our daughters,
how thrifty our sons!
How we've managed to fool the experts
in education, statistics and demography—
We're not very creative but not adverse to rote-learning.
Indeed, they can *use* us.
But the "Model Minority" is a tease.
We know you are watching now,
so we refuse to give you any!
Oh, bamboo shoots, bamboo shoots!
The further west we go, we'll hit east;
the deeper down we dig, we'll find China.
History has turned its stomach
on a black polluted beach—
where life doesn't hinge
on that red, red wheelbarrow,
but whether or not our new lover
in the final episode of "Santa Barbara"
will lean over a scented candle
and call us a "bitch."
Oh God, where have we gone wrong?
We have no inner resources!

.

Then, one redolent spring morning
the Great Patriarch Chin
peered down from his kiosk in heaven
and saw that his descendants were ugly.
One had a squarish head and a nose without a bridge.
Another's profile—long and knobbed as a gourd.
A third, the sad, brutish one
may never, never marry.
And I, his least favorite—

"not quite boiled, not quite cooked,"
a plump pomfret simmering in my juices—
too listless to fight for my people's destiny.
"To kill without resistance is not slaughter"
says the proverb. So, I wait for imminent death.
The fact that this death is also metaphorical
is testament to my lethargy.

.

So here lies Marilyn Mei Ling Chin,
married once, twice to so-and-so, a Lee and a Wong,
granddaughter of Jack "the patriarch"
and the brooding Suilin Fong,
daughter of the virtuous Yuet Kuen Wong
and G. G. Chin the infamous,
sister of a dozen, cousin of a million,
survived by everybody and forgotten by all.
She was neither black nor white,
neither cherished nor vanquished,
just another squatter in her own bamboo grove
minding her poetry—
when one day heaven was unmerciful,
and a chasm opened where she stood.
Like the jowls of a mighty white whale,
or the jaws of a metaphysical Godzilla,
it swallowed her whole.
She did not flinch nor writhe,
nor fret about the afterlife,
but stayed! Solid as wood, happily
a little gnawed, tattered, mesmerized
by all that was lavished upon her
and all that was taken away!

THE BARBARIANS ARE COMING

War chariots thunder, horses neigh, *the barbarians are coming.*
What are we waiting for, young nubile women pointing at the wall,
    the barbarians are coming.
They have heard about a weakened link in the wall. *So, the barbarians*
    have ears among us.
So deceive yourself with illusions: you are only one woman, holding one
    broken brick in the wall.
So deceive yourself with illusions: as if you matter, that brick and that wall.
The barbarians are coming: they have red beards or beardless with a top knot.
The barbarians are coming: they are your fathers, brothers, teachers, lovers;
    and they are clearly an other.
The barbarians are coming:
        If you call me a horse, I must be a horse.
        If you call me a bison, I am equally guilty.

When a thing is true and is correctly described, one doubles the blame by
    not admitting it: so, Zhuangzi, himself, was a barbarian king!
Horse, horse, bison, bison, *the barbarians are coming—*
and how they love to come.
The smells of the great frontier exult in them.

    after Cavafy

NEW YEAR'S LAMENT, 1988

A star falls and another poet dies—
in Manila, a stone came down
on her head like manna from heaven.
The newspaper said,
"She was a bad housewife, and besides,
her poetry wasn't lucid."
And Ai Qing, sweet uncle,
is three years gone. He bears witness now
only in an unfinished translation
collecting dust on my desk
and a thin aerogram pinned,
flapping on the wall.
Saying, "Dear Disciple,
you must never forgive them.
They have wasted my life!"
As the third world shakes
her tin roofs into the sun,
and the moon devours our Western elderberry,
I sit here on the eve of the revolution
in my inexpensive camisole
(the one that Santa brought me).
The joke is sad and is on me.
I scrawl this invective to you,
"a certain American poet,"
who has licked so many donkeys
that your tongue stays salty.
I will not lay my body down yet.
So, my lutestrings are broken,
and a giant cloud gathers rain over my piano.
The world left fallow will not be tilled—
each blade has been devoured,
each mote enslaved. Those we wish dead
will thrive past a hundred, those we esteem
will be sullied by thirty-three.

And I, once Guanyin's timid girlchild,
who teethed among the thieves
and suckled amidst the murderers—
I/we today are thirty-two.
As the rabbit sacrifices its tail
and escapes into the burrow,
the dragon appears, loud and sodden,
with a taste of cotton and thistle
in his ever lustful maw. And again,
he shall not have her!

Notes:
    Ai Qing: Chinese revolutionary and poet
    Kuan Yin: The Goddess of Mercy

BARBARIAN SUITE

for David Wong Louie

I.

The Ming will be over to make way for the Ch'ing.
The Ch'ing will be over to make way for eternity.
The East is red and the sun is rising.
All bleeds into the ocean in the Calafia west.
My loss is your loss, a dialect here, a memory there—
if my left hand is dying will my right hand cut it off?
We shall all be vestigial organs, the gift of democracy.
The pale faces, the wan conformity,
the price we pay for comfort is our mother tongue.

II.

China is an ocean away, our grandmother beaconing
with too many children, too many mouths to feed.
We can no longer dress her and improve her accent.
We can no longer toil in her restaurant "Double Happiness,"
    oiling woks, peeling shrimp.
She is the bridge—and we've broken her back with our weight.
We study Western philosophy and explore our raison d'être.
All is well in the suburbs when we are in love with poetry.

III.

What did ya think, the emperor will come to your grave?
To tell ya all is groovy in the hinterlands?
What did ya think? Life's that hunky-dory?
What did ya expect, old peasant, old fool,
one day out of the woods and the dirt will eject
    from your nostrils?
Even dung-heaps will turn fragrant with a thorough cleansing?

IV.

Orchids doth not bloom, baby, they cry, they explode.
Meanwhile our anger gets muted in their fatal beauty—

AmerAsia so harmonious under a canopy of stars.
The pram of a new nation, the winds rock it gently.
Truth has no face, we make it wear ours.
You walk on the beach with your beautiful son Julian.
We dare to eat peaches and discuss the classics.

V.

One day they came to me, my dead ancestors.
They whispered *sse-sse-sse,* homophonous with "death."
I was under the covers with my barbarian boyfriend,
blowing smoke rings, talking jazz—"Posterity"
is yet another "compromising position,"
    addenda to the Kama Sutra.
I was playing Goddess/Dominatress
and kept a piece of his ear as offering.

VI.

Cauldron full, cauldron empty.
The duck dangling in the window is the last vestige
    of our sizzling suzerainty.
They believed in order, which meant victory over oblivion.
They believed in the restaurant called "Double Happiness,"
where all the partners were brothers, all the sisters wore brocade.
The cash register rang its daily prayer wheels
    for the dying and the saved.

TURTLE SOUP

You go home one evening tired from work,
and your mother boils you turtle soup.
Twelve hours hunched over the hearth
(who knows what else is in that cauldron).

You say, "Ma, you've poached the symbol of long life;
that turtle lived four thousand years, swam
the Wei, up the Yellow, over the Yangtze.
Witnessed the Bronze Age, the High Tang,
grazed on splendid sericulture."
(So, she boils the life out of him.)

"All our ancestors have been fools.
Remember Uncle Wu who rode ten thousand miles
to kill a famous Manchu and ended up
with his head on a pole? Eat, child,
its liver will make you strong."

"Sometimes you're the life, sometimes the sacrifice."
Her sobbing is inconsolable.
So, you spread that gentle napkin
over your lap in decorous Pasadena.

Baby, some high priestess has got it wrong.
The golden decal on the green underbelly
says "Made in Hong Kong."

Is there nothing left but the shell
and humanity's strange inscriptions,
the songs, the rites, the oracles?

   for Ben Huang

SONG OF THE SAD GUITAR

In the bitter year of 1988 I was banished to San Diego, California, to become a wife there. It was summer. I was buying groceries under the Yin and Yang sign of Safeway. In the parking lot, the puppies were howling to a familiar tune on a guitar plucked with the zest and angst of the sixties. I asked the player her name.

She answered:

"Stone Orchid, but if you call me that, I'll kill you."

I said:

"Yes, perhaps stone is too harsh for one with a voice so pure."

She said:

"It's the 'Orchid' I detest; it's prissy, cliché and forever pink."

From my shopping bag I handed her a Tsing Tao and urged her to play on.

She sang about hitchhiking around the country, moons and lakes, homeward-honking geese, scholars who failed the examination. Men leaving for war; women climbing the watchtower. There were courts, more courts and inner-most courts, and scions who pillaged the country.

Suddenly, I began to feel deeply about my own banishment. The singer I could have been, what the world looked like in spring, that Motown collection I lost. I urged her to play on:

Trickle, Trickle, the falling rain.
Ming, ming, a deer lost in the forest.
Surru, surru, a secret conversation.
Hung, hung, a dog in the yard.

Then, she changed her mood, to a slower lament, trilled a song macabre, about death, about a guitar case that opened like a coffin. Each string vibrant, each note a thought. Tell me, Orchid, where are we going? "The book of changes does not signify change. The laws are immutable. Our fates are sealed." Said Orchid—the song is a dirge and an awakening.

Two years after our meeting, I became deranged. I couldn't cook, couldn't clean. My house turned into a pigsty. My children became delinquents. My husband began a long lusty affair with another woman. The house burned during a feverish *Santa Ana* as I sat in a pink cranny above the garage singing, "At twenty, I marry you. At thirty, I begin hating everything that you do."

One day while I was driving down Mulberry Lane, a voice came over the radio. It was Stone Orchid. She said, "This is a song for an old friend of mine. Her name is Mei Ling. She's a warm and sensitive housewife now living in Hell's Creek, California. I've dedicated this special song for her, 'The Song of the Sad Guitar.'"

I am now beginning to understand the song within the song, the weeping within the willow. And you, out there, walking, talking, seemingly alive—may truly be dead and waiting to be summoned by the sound of the sad guitar.

for Maxine Hong Kingston

THE DAO AND THE ART
OF LEAVETAKING

ALTAR

I tell her she has outlived her usefulness.
I point to the corner where dust gathers,
where light has never touched. But there she sits,
a thousand years, hands folded, in a tattered armchair,
with yesterday's news, "the Golden Mountain Edition."
The morning sun slants down the broken eaves,
shading half of her sallow face.

On the upper northwest corner (I'd consulted a geomancer),
a deathtrap shines on the dying bougainvillea.
The carcass of a goatmoth hangs upsidedown,
hollowed out. The only evidence
of her seasonal life is a dash
of shimmery powder, a last cry.

She, who was attracted to that bare bulb,
who danced around that immigrant dream,
will find her end here, this corner,
this solemn altar.

THE DAO AND THE ART OF LEAVETAKING

1)
Peach is prosaic: the object
has everyday applications.
Six globes of fruit, some
left on the sill too long.
Black on white, peduncles attached:
profound ontological statements—
nought, no, not nada, but nought.
Some may call it "nothingness,"
some prefer "pearapple," for
all fruits lead to God.

2)
Narcissus in a cracked porcelain bowl.
Chrysanthemum, mantis and gourd.
Crane and pine and wisteria.
Sparrow on a basket of persimmons.
Still-life with peaches and plum blossoms.
Landscape with pavillions and pomegranates.
Touchable and turbid—speakable and nameable.

3)
Emptiness is but one mind.
One mind is of no mind.
Observe the technique,
ponder in it—
        become
a wooden doll with no ego—
it thinks nothing, it does nothing.
Let legs splay and arms flail.
Discipline is the ultimate freedom—
take off her head, open, see: hollow.

4)
Practice the fine delineations:
the subtle nuances, distinctions
clear-cut as a hair—
Though you died you have to let me go.
Though I died I must let you go.
Though she died, still, we must go.
Though he died she must go.

5)
What is above the form is the Tao.
What is within the form is called "tools."
That which transforms things is called "change."
I see you walking in your newly hennaed hair,
gingerly, a monk treading on rice paper.
I see you dancing in your Hawaiian-flowered shirt.

6)
My dark skin against your whiteness,
a winter sky that resists the dawn.
Leavetaking at its simplest—
last night the verses halted,
the rice paper lay idle.
The black ink dried in the receptacle.

A BREAK IN THE RAIN
(or: Shall we meet again on Angel Island?)

Better Squat

Better squat than sit—
    sitting is too comfortable.
Better squat than stand—
    standing is too expectant.
Better squat and wait—
    as many have done before you,
head bent, knees hugged, body curled.

Better play

And after all,
it is only Ping-Pong,
a game,
one to a side,
fixed points & boundaries,
a net that divides.
You needn't talent
or money,
only a green table
& white balls.
At first you play at the Y,
perhaps later
at Julie's or Mary's
in a freshly paneled room,
should you be invited.

Better dance

With the one named Rochester
who likes your kind.
Let us dub him
"the point of entry."

Suddenly, he notices
your latticed hair.

Better Wait

The queues are long
& the amenities spare.

But *do* play.
Play,
dance, sing,
wait for a break in the rain.

REGGAE RENGA

A man flat on his back can't go to the doctor.

.

Let him die, woman, so that he will no longer beat you.

.

He says, "Meet me at the hallowed temple near the Buddha's topknot."

.

He is dying, dying fast. In his delirium he is ever so beautiful.

.

I am late and reach only as far as the earlobes where I hear he has gone.

.

There are trees on the mountains and branches on the trees.

.

My anger so clear—I can see the hairs on the caterpillar and the wind
    on the hairs.

.

I can tell the paths that he has violated by the bent lay of the grasses.

.

Within him is a worm that loves itself and forgets whom he is loving,
    his mouth or his asshole.

.

Near the tombstone is a plum tree; a cock crows upon it, saying,
    "Man, you are no good!"

.

The people of my country are baleful; they've sent me to accuse you!

.

What is your ailment, wretched white, your ailment, will no birds sing?

SAKURA, PAINTER

I ask how she has come
to this predilection
for horror and not love:

(translation)
Well, it happened when I was a child:
happy among the cherry boughs,
spoiled by mimosa milk and Ikebana lessons,
I met my first lover who opened his balaclava
to a double-edged sword. I thought I was in love.
You see, this was Japan the empire and what
was understood as love.

Then, came her "Oeuvre: Visions and Manifestoes."
A spear through the heart of Goya,
Mishima's Appaloosas bloodying the snow,
headless Madonnas—no icon escapes the brush,
the knife, the death throes.

If you were a painter, would you be a woman less savage?
Oh, Sakura, forgive these platitudes, these camellias.

ELEGY FOR CHLOE NGUYEN

(1955–1988)

Chloe's father is a professor of linguistics.
Mine runs a quick-you-do-it Laundromat in Chinatown.
If not pretty, at least I'm clean.

Bipedal in five months, trilingual in a year,
at eleven she had her first lover.

Here's a photo of Chloe's mother in the kitchen
making *petit fours, petit fours* that are very pretty.
Here's my mother picking pears, picking pears
for a self-made millionaire grower.

The night when Chloe died, her father sighed,
"Chloe was my heart; Chloe was my life!"

One day under an earthen black sky
and the breeze brushing our adolescent pinafores,
a star fell—or was it a satellite
exploding into a bonfire at the horizon?
Chloe said, "This is how I want to die,
with a bang and not with a flicker."

Oh, Chloe, eternally sophomore and soporific!
Friend of remote moribund languages!
Chloe read Serbo-Croatian, the Latin of Horace.
She understood Egyptian hieroglyphics, the writing of the tombs.
The tongues of the living, the slangs of the dead—
in learning she had no rival.

Then came the lovers of many languages
to quell her hunger, her despair.

Each night they whispered, "Chloe, you are beautiful."
Then left her with an empty sky in the morning.

Chloe, can you hear me? Is it better in heaven?
Are you happier in hell? This week I don't understand the lesson
being a slow learner—except for the one about survival.
And Death, I know him well . . .

He followed my grandfather as a puff of opium,
my father as a brand new car.
Rowed the boat with my grandmother,
blowing gales into my mother's ear.
Wrapped his arms around my asthmatic sister,
but his comforting never won us over.

Yes, Death is a beautiful man,
and the poor don't need dowries to court him.
His grassy hand, his caliph—you thought you could master.

Chloe, we are finally Americans now. Chloe, we are here!

LEAVING SAN FRANCISCO

The coldest winter's day I remember
was a summer's night in San Francisco.
An old hoary sage-poet said something like that.
But if you live here you must don a new layer
and let the consequences take over.

No, this is not Xian, where the peasants sold you
Qin's tomb for a dollar. No, this is not Kaifeng
where the poets ate cinnabar to become immortals.
The connubial geese have stopped migrating;
they've settled on a stagnant tarn near Anza Terrace.

The Bay swells with winter and waits for a reprieve.
This spring the sun will heal the wound on your head
and you'll be famous for a moment. Alone in the motel room
you recite to an audience of one. The crack clambering
the wall deserves a villanelle if not a sestina.

But the Goddess of Mercy is weary; she averts her eyes,
as the demon's dark hand grips us, dragging our regrets
deep into the bay with the bottomfish.
If I float a poem over the Golden Gate Bridge,
Master Weldon, will you answer?

for Weldon Kees

SAD GUITAR

(Sad Guitar series #3/3)

Blind immigrant,
do you understand this:
touch, wood,
this is wood
and not fire, this
earth and not wood.
This is elemental water.

.

Tea brews, rice boils,
ten days since your departure.
I stagger, stumble,
let old associations go.
What rhymes with flower,
bower, shower, power?

.

Stranger, have you ever loved
a Chinese woman?
Her heart is chrysanthemum.
And there are deeper chasms.

.

Oh, the goads, the rancor!
here I am within you, without you,
groping the fleshy dark,
conjuring the spirits and the furies.

.

I am a woman without rope
chasing a runaway horse
whose chariots neigh
and hoofbeats plunder.

.

I hear you, but I don't see you.
I touch you, but you seem far.
What I have learned about loneliness
is the three fingers that strum
the heart of the all-knowing—
the dark pith of the sad guitar.

AUTUMN LEAVES

The dead piled up, thick, fragrant, on the fire escape.
My mother ordered me again, and again, to sweep it clean.
All that blooms must fall. I learned this not from the Dao,
    but from high school biology.

Oh, the contradictions of having a broom and not a dustpan!
I swept the leaves down, down through the iron grille
and let the dead rain over the Wong family's patio.

And it was Achilles Wong who completed the task.
    We called her:
The-one-who-cleared-away-another-family's-autumn.
She blossomed, tall, benevolent, notwithstanding.

THE PHOENIX GONE,
THE TERRACE EMPTY

CLEAR WHITE STREAM

Clear white stream—
a dead horse drifts;
its legs are branches
piercing the sky.

Clear white stream—
a child dangles her pole;
deep in the water
a lungfish bites.

Clear white stream—
a man mooring a boat;
his cormorant is diving
with rope around its gullet.

Clear white stream—
a ripe red sun
drags its head
across the hollyhock.

Clear white stream—
how all will pass:
days and nights,
one horse's demise.

Clear white stream—
above my forehead
blue flies tarry
around a naked bulb.

Clear white stream—
am I river or horse,
man or cormorant,
woman or child?

Am I Zhuangzi's bad dream
shorn of an awakening?

THE PHOENIX GONE, THE TERRACE EMPTY

川 流 不 息

The river flows without ceasing

Shallow river, shallow river,
these stairs are steep,
one foot, another,
I gather the hem
of my terry-cloth robe.
Quietly,
gingerly,
if an inch could sing
I would sing
for miles—
past the courtyard,
past the mulberries,
past the Bodhi tree
fragrant with jossticks,
past the Buddha
whose laughter is unmerciful.
Saunter,
my pink horses,
my tiny soldiers.
Heartbeat, hoofbeat,
softly,
gingerly,
do not disturb
the nasturtium,
do not ruin the irises
they planted.
In the rock garden
the flagstones
caress my feet,
kiss them tenderly.

"Who in the netherworld
walks on my soles

as I walk?
And opens her black mouth
when I cry?
Whose lutestrings
play my sorrow?
Whose silence
undulates
a millenium
of bells,
in which
all of history
shall wallow?"

This banister
painted with red lacquer
where
my grip turns white.
These plum blossoms,
stock signifiers,
mocking my own ripeness
I cannot taste.
Flesh remembers
what the mind resists.
I think of
love
or the warm blur,
my mother—
I remember hate,
the hard shape,
my father.
They, slow moving,
mugworts,
no, water bison,
discuss my future
in a fulcrum
of angry gestures.
They shall come,
they shall come,

for our tithes.
She, my grandmother,
oiling her shuttle,
sings a lullaby
in an ancient falsetto,
In the east, a pink sash,
a girl has run away
from her mother.
He, my grandfather,
itinerant tinker,
heaves
his massive bellows.
His ember of hope flickering
in the village's
eternal sepulchre.
Do you remember
the shanty towns
on the hills of Wanchai,
tin roofs
crying into the sun?
Do you remember
mother's first lover,
hurling
a kerosene lamp
into a hovel?
Ooooh, I can smell
the charred sweetness
in his raven hair.
The hills ablaze
with mayflies
and night-blooming jasmine.

Open the gate,
open,
the gilded facade
of restaurant "Double Happiness."
The man crouched

on the dirty linoleum
fingering dice
is my father.
He says:
"Mei Ling, child,
Mei Ling, don't cry,
I can change our lives
with one strike."

Do you know the stare
of a dead man?
My father the ox,
without his yoke,
sitting on a ridge
of the quay.
Auntie Jade
remembers:
"Hunger
had spooned
the flesh
from his cheeks.
His tuft
of black hair
was his only movement.
That Chinaman
had no ideals,
no beliefs,
his dreams
were robbed
by the Japanese,
his fortune
was plundered
by the Nationalists,
the Communists
seared his home.
Misery had propped
him there.

When you pray
to your ancestors
you are praying
to his hollowness."
Amaduofu, amaduofu—
child, child
they cried,
"Ten thousand years of history and you have come to this.
Four thousand years of tutelage and you have come to this!"

Shall I walk
into the new world
in last year's pinafore?
Chanel says:
black, black
is our century's color.
Proper and elegant,
slim silhouette,
daywear and nightwear,
for parties and death,
and deep, deep regret.

"So, you've come home
finally
with your new boyfriend.
What is his name?
Ezekiel!
Odd name for a boy.
Your mother can't pronounce it.
And she doesn't like
his demeanor.
Too thin, too sallow,
he does not eat beef
in a country
where beef is possible.
He cannot play the violin
in a country

where rapture is possible.
He beams a tawdry smile,
perhaps he is hiding
bad intentions.
And that Moon
which accompanied his arrival,
that Moon won't drink
and is shaped naughtily
like a woman's severed ear."

The snake bites her own tail,
meaning harmony at the year's end.
Or does it mean
she is eating herself
into extinction?

Oh dead prince, Oh hateful love,
shall we meet again
on the bridge of magpies?
Will you kiss me tenderly
where arch meets toe meets ankle,
where dried blood warbles?

Little bird, little bird,
something escaping,
something escaping . . .

The phoenix gone, the terrace empty.
Look, Mei Ling,
yellow crowfoot in the pond,
not lotus, not lily.

HOW WE SAVED THE OTHER

to the beat of a Tartar drum

Down, all down, south of the morass,
not Alabama, Mississippi,
but south—Pacific, subtropics,
and Auntie Jade is young again.
Her skin is brown and her heart is the soil.

As we, sisters: Ah Jen, Ah Ling, Ah Lan,
young as sprigs and fresh in the loins,
eat mangoes, passions, papaya,
almond grassjelly and guava.
The ice is from Manila.
The blender from America.

So Auntie cracks the coconut
and finds the milk.
She feeds my sisters,
but I am allergic.

So Auntie lowers the machete
and cuts the cane.
The cane is young;
it bleeds milksap
onto my tongue.

And the milk is tasty,
the milk is good.
And all of us dance
the way that children do,
the rain thundering over.

Then down, down the mountain
comes the other.
She is baleful,
she is spent,

her heart in a fist,
her long plait unwound,
and she cries, cries:
don't let them take me!

The sisters love magnolias,
the magnolias are red,
we peel their skirts
to release the flurries.
And we drum,
sticks to barrel,
duster to tin can,
dry ice in the blender.

Way beyond the jalousies,
way beyond the lairs,
the men—disguised in forest—come;
they run, run, run
after her.

MOON AND OATGRASS

The moon is not over the water,
as you would have it,
but one with it, and the house
is on the precipice
overlooking a green meadow.
And you—an *eye* and not an *I*—
are walking through it.

And whether you live here
or are visiting
in your long pilgrimage—
is my prerogative.
Whether she is your acolyte,
the Pearl Concubine,
or a mere beggarwoman—
is also my invention.

Only I know where
terrace ends and house begins,
whether the country is lost,
whether rivers and mountains
will continue. And finally,

after the inkstone is dry,
we shall be together
high in a corner bedroom
with a pale view of hills.
Without pleasure or transcendence
we penetrate this landscape.

And what *is* this landscape?
The moon in oatgrass,
the oatgrass moon.
A woman pacing
the linoleum floor,

contemplating a poem.
A man dissolving
into the dailiness of rain

and the red eye of morning.

THE GILDED CANGUE

(Phoenix series #2/3)

For moments we forget the sound her lotus feet make,
the scurry of a fawn, delicate and hesitant.
The pain in her small hooves pursed her lips,
a secret she never told us.

When we ventured into her innermost room
we found her warm impression
coiled as a serial conch
on the silken divan
and a pinkness raw
as the frail life that dwelled within.

In dream we saw her fly into the sky
and dance on the bridge of magpies—
nobody to restrain her on earth,
nobody to call her back
in the courtyard, at the watermargin.

What is poetry if it could forget
the meaning of her life?
Her long hair let go only once
on that breezy terrace,
a smile so faint as to mock her own death.

All suffering forestalled freedom.
The gilded cangue opened, her final escape—
now, you and I must descend.

HOMAGE TO DIANA TOY

Crestwood Psychiatric Hospital, 1983

GRUEL

Your name is Diana Toy.
And all you may have for breakfast is rice gruel.
You can't spit it back into the cauldron for it would be unfilial.
You can't ask for yam gruel for there is none.
You can't hide it in the corner for it would surely be found,
and then you would be served cold, stale rice gruel.

This is the philosophy of your tong:
you, the child, must learn to understand the universe
through the port-of-entry, your mouth,
to discern bitter from sweet, pungent from bland.
You were told that the infant Buddha once devoured earth
and spewed forth the wisdom of the ages.

Meat or gruel, wine or ghee,
even if it's gruel, even if it's nothing,
that gruel, that nothingness will shine
into the oil of your mother's scrap-iron wok,
into the glare of your father's cleaver,
and dance in your porcelain bowl.

Remember, what they deny you won't hurt you.
What they spare you, you must make shine,
so shine, shine . . .

THE DISORDER

The only truth you know now is your hunger
growing wider as the season darkens.
And all the fasting and Hindu calisthenics
couldn't keep those inches off. The fat
adheres to you like cancer or a warm lichen
dependent on a tree trunk's insecurity
and unwilling to part.
                            Everywhere
you venture the mirrors whisper,
the pond's reflections resound your dolor.
The winter doldrums comfort the beasts
within all but yourself—
                            As you reach out
to gather more confections and sweet rewards,
As you attempt to fill an emptiness
not filled by the sun, as you wait
for your inevitable fall,
                            a small child
within you remembers: *so, these, these*
were the "golden mountains!"

DIANA TAKES A NAP; DOLORES CALLS
MIA TO APOLOGIZE; MRS. MOOREHEAD
LEAVES FOR THE COMMUNITY

.

After you get well, Diana,
we'll take that long drive.
You know there will be many chances:
like rain that falls on the flowers
and the sun coming through,
again and again, after the rain.
But today, there are particulars:
bath-time, nap-time, music therapy,
a meeting to condemn contrabands.
Mr. Sebastian has grievances.
Mrs. Moorehead is leaving for the community.

.

And so—she acquiesces to a shower.
"I am a princess," she says,
"like Yang Gueifei,
I have skin like a lily's.
Lilies don't shower;
they stay pink and pretty in the sun,
pink and pretty."

I pat-dry her dark, frail body,
rub balm into a trail of purplish bedsores.

"Camellias," I say to myself,
"Camellias, not lilies."

.

Three o'clock: nap for the masses.
And I am finally free
for a fifteen-minute hiatus
to think of my own.
I call my daughter on the pay phone:

"Hello, hello, darling Mia,
listen, about yesterday,
I didn't mean to embarrass you
in front of Jeremy Lyons.
I am human. I get tired.
From now on, you are your own woman,
run with the rainbow if you desire,
but never regret the road you have chosen,
for there is no way back to the womb."

.

Nobody ever goes home to Canton.
The girl, her dog, her dreams.
So, Mrs. Moorehead is finally ready.
As hoary-headed as Tu Fu,
she embarks on her first journey.
One small step, another, she walks
gingerly out the door, turns, waves:
"Ladies and gentlemen, I hope
we meet again, only this time
on the other side of the wall."

.

Diana, Mia, there is new life in the tundra.
No matter how insignificant, how small,
she cries out from the blearing sun
with the same love of life, the same vengeance.
The god that placed you in this world
placed you in mine; so, brandish your copper bracelets!
My number has seven paltry digits.
You have a good memory. So dial, call.
My work is not finished until the moon fades in my eyes,
and even then, even then . . .

FIRST LESSONS, REDUX

It is not the hunter who is cunning
but the hunted who has learned
to dash into that familiar hole
until the dogs pass.

It is not the gun cocked
or the fingers caressing the trigger
that makes us march
somnambulantly on.

There is no guiding light from heaven,
for I can hear the blind ox
tapping her foot in the darkness
to find the path.

It is not the pottage but the cauldron
that is our enchantment—
mother's flesh and father's dictum
our succor. And Diana,

the eyes between her ancestors and the world,
was studying to become a citizen
in early August ember.
And I, her unworthy tutor,

failed to tell her about the fifty paltry stars
that amount to a little more
than sensible graphics
and fine accounting.

And despite my tutelage
somebody had drafted her purpose,

stamped "destination: elsewhere,"
and "re-entry denied."

My last glimpse of her
was a bad, impish drawing
pinned—a hollow specimen—
flapping on the wall.

What will be remembered
of that summer lesson
but a moth dying on the screen,
leaving her face-powder.

THE ADMINISTRATOR

The women are within her, smoking angel dust, sipping tea,
when, suddenly, he enters with his chest bare. He
from the other world of slender black ties and shiny shoes—
the keeper of the gate, the purveyor of keys. He says,
"You would not bite the hand that feeds you, Diana." And so,
she succumbs to him . . . and those within chant the song of the prairie:
the beast does what beasts do as the lion plays with his maw,
and the carrion teases the condor. In the morning, he walks
down the dim corridor and greets her, as always, in his
official tone, high and horselike. "Good morning, Diana,
did you have a good sleep?" And she ponders the meaning
of sleep—A skeleton pushing a gondola across the water. When
will she reach the other side? Will there be lions in wait?
Pills to swallow? Papers to sign? From across his large white desk
he opens his leather-bound files. Again, again chant the witnesses,
The state is your conservator; the prairie will be your life!

ITS NAME

These hands are small, Diana,
they can fix only what is before them.
This mosaic is difficult to piece.
The corners aren't fashioned to fit.
Snow White's face has been defiled,
and some dwarves are lost.

If I were a good soldier, if I were free
to love you as a sister,
I would take you home; and we
would live happily ever after
in my tiny, mother-in-law apartment
in the city, in the woods.

A new cricket is in the cage
and is not singing, but you
believe that it can sing
and have heard its aria. There
is a thin tag on its left leg.
Its name: 20901, Maria.

THE SURVIVOR

Don't tap your chopsticks against your bowl.
Don't throw your teacup against the wall in anger.
Don't suck on your long black braid and weep.
Don't tarry around the big red sign that says "danger!"

All the tempests will render still; seas will calm,
horses will retreat, voices to surrender.

.

That you have bloomed this way and not that,
that your skin is yellow, not white, not black,
that you were born not a boychild but a girl,
that this world will be forever puce-pink are just as well.

Remember, the survivor is not the strongest or most clever;
merely, the survivor is almost always the youngest.
And you shall have to relinquish that title before long.

ALBA

White moon, white blossoms, white milky way,
White, white, morning of December.
Last night's candle has burned to a nub,
But she does not need another;
The snow outside her window is her guiding light.
Diana yearns to follow the old masters now,
Cuts four parallel lines into her heart.
You ask: why not a peony or a harmonious rainbow?
For the pattern of death should be exacting
As the rituals of life. So, do not mourn her.
You never shed a tear into her tin cup of living.
Tears would be spit now on the grave of the dead.

LOVE POESY

(Where is the moralizer, your mother?)

OLD ASIAN HAND

Old Asian hand,
touch me where it flutters,
my heart, my body's butterfly,
one violet camellia,
pulses in the dead of night.

Old Asian hand,
the moon gnaws your left side.
Yellow are the grasses
that never learned to writhe.

Old Asian hand,
below the blue equator, have you discovered
the warm, moist lichen
of early autumn?

Beneath the marl of the new diaspora,
clear water runs.

ODE TO PRIZED KOI AND BABY FINCHES

The moon was up.
He kept climbing, offering me
faint cattleyas, mums
and dyed-blue asters.
Mother from the second story
cried:
    Don't break her cherry blossoms!
Father tied our Doberman
around the elm, saying:
    Don't make the dog bark!
and sister watched forlornly
through a break in the fence.

. . . .

Grandmother received me in Guangtung
and found my umbilical cord
wrapped in rice paper.
My name and birthright were inscribed
by her faded, grassy hand.

Child, promise me that all would continue:
our race, our name, our tong,
our dialect, our heritage, our God!

. . . .

Upon entering the world—
    there would be no return.

Upon treading the path—
    there would be no detours.

When one plum ripens—
    the others will follow.

I say to my sister, *Hold on, baby, hold on,*
    be that one plum that resists falling!

. . . .

Ode to my prized koi and baby finches:
please forgive my arrogance,
but to be human means to never look back.
The lost country of my birth,
the forbidden lovers in the moon,
the broken promises in my heart
give me a sadness that you would never know
being merely, happily, fish and fowl.

WHERE IS THE MORALIZER, YOUR MOTHER?

1)
A child in the courtyard is serious in her game.
She avoids a crack
lest she break her mother's back.
She sidesteps a line
to preserve her mother's spine.

2)
I dreamt of the Goddess of Mercy floating in the estuary.
Did you not see her there,
vertical among the eelgrass?
The pale one, was it not she,
the one with the small forehead?

3)
Roberto, are you sleeping,
or just pretending to be asleep?
Your eyes neither open nor closed:
half-black in the netherworld,
half-green in longing.

4)
I shall love you into eternity.
Eternity as in a fly
drinking sleep from an infant's eye.
Eternity as in its leg,
black and bent,
mocking the universe.

5)
Where is the door to the bedroom?
Mei Ling, where is the moralizer,
your mother? She was walking in
as you were walking out.

6)
Again, again, we tell them our story.
Once upon a time:
he was thirty-three,
she, 4987, not counting
the earlier stages of the Shang.

7)
Or:
In the forest, a dead deer lies,
bound up with string.
In the forest, a dead deer lies,
bound up with string.

8)
My mother is tired
and deep in her sartorial woods;
she has no eyes to scowl,
no ears to eavesdrop,
no voice to berate me now.

URBAN LOVE POEM

1)
Condominium, stiff bamboo,
refuses to bend in the wind,
squats in the sinking earth
like a thin-hipped dowager.
You arrange the amenities
and we pay the rent. So, please,
don't fall as civilizations fall
in the comfort of night.

2)
Gingko, vomit-eater of the metropolis,
city's oxygen, small men's shadow,
your gentle bark can't protect you now.
One pellicle, another, falls
on the land of your displacement.
Where is the Yellow Emperor who nurtured you?
Where is your birthplace,
the Yangtze, the Pearl?

3)
Hong Kong, San Francisco, San Jose,
the path through the "Golden Mountains"
is a three-tiered freeway. Look up:
it suspends where no prophet can touch.
A quick fix in your veins; a white rush in my mind—
you cry, "Mei Ling, Mei Ling, once
we could've had everything:
the talent, the courage, the wherewithal."

4)
Oh, the small delectables of day:
persimmons from Chinatown,
a stroll through the Tenderloin
with the man I love.

My darling, please, don't be sad.
I've parked my horse
in this gray, gray sunrise
to gather sweet crocuses and jonquils
for you.

HIS PARENTS' BAGGAGE

When we first met he had nothing,
naked as a brand-new lamb.
Fresh dew shimmered on the wool of his back.
Then, slowly, my small apartment filled
with meaningful gimcrack of his past.
And then, his parents' baggage . . .

First, his mother's small leathers:
prim, expensive, with a good name,
filled to the brim, ready to explode.
Took three friends to sit them closed.

Then his father's soft naugahyde:
one special piece, a suit-bag hung
over the doorjamb like a fresh carcass
picked open by private vultures.
And he and his sisters were the last
worms to clean the ribs.

I beg the question: who is host, who is guest?
Who the eater, who the eaten?
And in the depth of night,
in the wake of our dreams,
I reach out my arms to embrace what is left.

AND ALL I HAVE IS TU FU

Pied horse, pied horse, I am having a dream.
Twenty-five Mongolians on horseback, twenty-five;
their hooves gouging deep trenches into the loess.
Now they enter a hole in the Wall, now they retreat.
Freud snickers; Jung shakes his head.

Then, a soldier comes forward who calls himself Tu Fu.
He opens his mouth and issues a cartouche:
all black-bearded, knitted-browed,
each meaning "what your viscera look like
after having been disemboweled!"

Pray, promise me, this is not what the dream portends—
my roommate's in the bathroom fucking my boyfriend,
and all I have is Tu Fu.

COMPOSED NEAR THE BAY BRIDGE

(after a wild party)

1)
Amerigo has his finger on the pulse of China.
He, Amerigo, is dressed profoundly punk:
Mohawk-pate, spiked dog collar, black leather thighs.
She, China, freshly hennaed and boaed, is intrigued
with the new diaspora and the sexual freedom
called *bondage.* "Isn't *bondage,* therefore,
a *kind* of freedom?" she asks, wanly.

2)
Thank God there was no war tonight.
Headbent, Amerigo plucks his bad guitar.
The Sleeping Giant snores with her mouth agape
while a lone nightingale trills on a tree.

Through the picture window, I watch the traffic
hone down to a quiver. Loneliness. Dawn.
A few geese winging south; minor officials return home.

SUMMER LOVE

The black smoke rising means that I am cooking
dried lotus, bay oysters scrambled with eggs.
If this doesn't please you, too bad, it's all I have.
I don't mind your staying for breakfast—but, please—do not linger;
nothing worse in the morning than last night's love.

Your belly is flat and your skin—milk in the moonlight.
I notice your glimmer among a thousand tired eyes.
When we dance closely, fog thickens, all distinctions falter.
I let you touch me where I am most vulnerable,
heart of the vulva, vulva of the heart.

Perhaps, I fear, there will not be another like you.
Or you might walk away in the same face of the others—
    —blue with scorn and a troubled life.
But, for now, let the summers be savored and the centuries be forgiven.
Two lovers in a field of floss and iris—
where nothing else matters but the dew and the light.

BEIJING SPRING

for the Chinese Democratic Movement

NEW CHINA

In youth I had nothing
that warned me of heaven's vagaries.
My nature always
was to love the hills and waters.
Then, suddenly, I plunged
into the squalid pitfall, the world.
Once having fallen
it would be forty-two years—
the worm must dig deeper now to find the light.

· · · · · · ·

Yet, my caged canary
yearns to sing in the forest.
The fattened koi in my pond
dreams of the ocean.

And I, their master, must one day set them free.
No grief nor joy greater than this one.

THE FLORAL APRON

The woman wore a floral apron around her neck,
that woman from my mother's village
with a sharp cleaver in her hand.
She said, "What shall we cook tonight?
Perhaps these six tiny squid
lined up so perfectly on the block?"

She wiped her hand on the apron,
pierced the blade into the first.
There was no resistance,
no blood, only cartilage
soft as a child's nose. A last
iota of ink made us wince.

Suddenly, the aroma of ginger and scallion fogged our senses,
and we absolved her for that moment's barbarism.
Then, she, an elder of the tribe,
without formal headdress, without elegance,
deigned to teach the younger
about the Asian plight.

And although we have traveled far
we must never forget that primal lesson
—on patience, courage, forbearance,
on how to love squid despite squid,
how to honor the village, the tribe,
that floral apron.

AGAINST WAR, AGAINST WATCHTOWER

My cousin is wearing blunt bangs across her forehead—
　　a bowl cut, for her mother was cruel.

My cousin is sitting behind a trellis of honeysuckle—playing
　　with green plums. Oh, when will she finally eat them?

You should have seen her tremble when the boys walked by
　　shouldering their radios.

You should have seen her run across my courtyard and vanish
　　into the mulberry—crying with shame.

I am sitting behind my high window with a clear view of hills.

I am sitting behind my gauze curtains waiting for the rebellion to be over.

I am parting my curtains slowly to beacon them with long fingers.

Come, come, my darlings, welcome into my visage, my terror.

TIENANMEN, THE AFTERMATH

There was blood and guts all over the road.
I said I'm sorry, darling, and rolled over,
expecting the slate to be clean; but she came,
she who was never alive became resurrected.
I saw her in dream . . . a young girl in a *qipao*,
bespeckled, forever lingering, thriving
on the other side of the world, walking in my soles
as I walk, crying in my voice as I cried. When
she arrived, I felt my knuckles in her knock,
her light looming over the city's great hollows.

Hope lies within another country's semaphores.
The Goddess of Liberty, the Statue of Mercy—
we have it all wrong—big boy, how we choose to love,
how we choose to destroy, says Zhuangzi is written
in heaven—but leave the innocent ones alone,
those alive, yet stillborn, undead, yet waiting
in a fitful sleep undeserved of an awakening.

IS IT SNOWING IN GUANGZHOU?

1)
Is this too dark?
I mean—my new henna.

Is this too pale?
This fresh makeup
that comes off on my pillow.

Is this too coy?
"I part my gauze curtains slowly."

Should I tell you my name?
The familial and the diminuitive.

2)
Is this a metaphor?
"A red-naped insect."

And this?
"A woman walking like a line of ancient waka into the rain."

Is "Black-eyed Susans on a hillock"—
the collective unconscious?

3)
Where is my jade hairpin?
My, aren't you a materialist!

Where is my jade hairpin?
I gave it away; your grandmother will be angry.

Where is my jade hairpin?
If you've borrowed it, please return it!

Then, in turn, I shall return it

back to the Spring and Autumn period
from whence it came.

4)
Is it snowing in Guangzhou?
No, friend, never
in the southernmost province.

Is it snowing in Heilongjiang?
How do I know, I have never been there.

Is it snowing in Beijing?
In that little lane named *Fangfa*.

Note:
> *fangfa*—double entendre, meaning:
> 1) method, the way of doing things
> 2) the blossoming of flowers

BEIJING SPRING

Love, if I could give you the eternal summer sun
or China back her early ideological splendor, I would.
If I could hoist the dead horses back
and retrieve the wisdom charred by the pyres of Qin.
If I could give Mother the Hong Kong of her mulberry youth
and Father the answers that the ox desired,
they would still be together now and not blame
their sadness on the unyieldy earth.
If I had separated goose from gander, goose from gander,
the question of monogamy and breeding for life, the question
of the pure yellow seed would not enter.

This courtyard, this fortress,
this alluvium where the dead leave their faces—
each step I take erases the remnants of another,
each song I sing obfuscates the song of Changan,
ripples washing sand ripples washing sand ripples . . .
each poem I write conjures the dead washing-women of Loyang.

Lover, on Tienanmen Square, near the Avenue of Eternal Peace,
I believe in the passions of youth,
I believe in eternal spring.
As the white blossoms, sweet harbingers,
pull a wreath around the city,
as heaven spreads its blue indifference over
the bloodied quay, I want to hold you
against the soft silhouettes of my people.
Let me place my mouth over your mouth,
let me breathe life into your life,
let me summon the paired connubial geese
from the far reaches of the galaxy
to soar over the red spokes of the sun's slow chariot
and begin again.

A PORTRAIT OF THE SELF AS NATION, 1990–1991

> Fit in dominata servitus
> In servitude dominatus
> *In mastery there is bondage*
> *In bondage there is mastery*
> (Latin proverb)

> *The stranger and the enemy*
> *We have seen him in the mirror.*
> (George Seferis)

Forgive me, Head Master,
but you see, I have forgotten
to put on my black lace underwear, and instead
I have hiked my slip up, up to my waist
so that I can enjoy the breeze.
It feels good to be *without,*
so good as to be salacious.
The feeling of flesh kissing tweed.
If ecstasy had a color, it would be
yellow and pink, yellow and pink
Mongolian skin rubbed raw.
The serrated lining especially fine
like wearing a hair-shirt, inches above the knee.
When was the last time I made love?
The last century? With a wan missionary.
Or was it San Wu the Bailiff?
The tax collector who came for my tithes?
The herdboy, the ox, on the bridge of magpies?
It was Roberto, certainly,
high on coke, circling the galaxy.
Or my recent vagabond love
driving a reckless chariot, lost
in my feral country. *Country,* Oh I am

so punny, so very, very punny.
Dear Mr. Decorum, don't you agree?

It's not so much the length of the song
but the range of the emotions—Fear
has kept me a good pink monk—and poetry
is my nunnery. Here I am alone in my altar,
self-hate, self-love, both self-erotic notions.
Eyes closed, listening to that one hand clapping—
not metaphysical trance, but fleshly mutilation—
and loving *it,* myself and that pink womb, my bed.
Reading "Jing Pingmei" in the "expurgated"
where all the female protagonists were named
Lotus.
Those damned licentious women named us
Modest, Virtue, Cautious, Endearing,
Demure-dewdrop, Plum-aster, Petal-stamen.
They teach us to walk headbent in devotion,
to honor the five relations, ten sacraments.
Meanwhile, the feast is brewing elsewhere,
the ox is slaughtered and her entrails are hung
on the branches for the poor. They convince us, yes,
our chastity will save the nation—Oh mothers,
all your sweet epithets didn't make us wise!
Orchid by any other name is equally seditious.

Now, where was I, oh yes, now I remember,
the last time I made love, it was to *you.*
I faintly remember your whiskers
against my tender nape.
You were a conquering barbarian,
helmeted, halberded,
beneath the gauntleted moon,
whispering Hunnish or English—
so-long Oolong went the racist song,

bye-bye little chinky butterfly.
There is no cure for self-pity,
the disease is death,
ennui, disaffection,
a roll of flesh-colored tract homes crowding my imagination.
I do hate my loneliness,
sitting cross-legged in my room,
satisfied with a few off-rhymes,
sending off precious haiku to some inconspicuous journal
named "Left Leaning Bamboo."
You, my precious reader, O sweet voyeur,
sweaty, balding, bespeckled,
in a rumpled rayon shirt
and a neo-Troubadour chignon,
politics mildly centrist,
the *right* fork for the *right* occasions,
matriculant of the best schools—
herewith, my last confession
(with decorous and perfect diction)
I loathe to admit. Yet, I shall admit it:
there was no Colonialist coercion;
sadly, we blended together well.
I was poor, starving, war torn,
an empty coffin to be filled,
You were a young, ambitious Lieutenant
with dreams of becoming Prince
of a "new world order," Lord
over the League of Nations.

Lover, destroyer, savior!
I remember that moment of beguilement,
one hand muffling my mouth,
one hand untying my sash—
On your throat dangled a golden cross.
Your god is jealous, your god is cruel.
So, when did you finally return?
And . . . was there a second coming?
My memory is failing me, perhaps

you came too late
(we were already dead).
Perhaps you didn't come at all—
you had a deadline to meet,
another alliance to secure,
another resistance to break.
Or you came too often
to my painful dismay.
(Oh, how facile the liberator's hand.)
Often when I was asleep
You would hover over me
with your great silent wingspan
and watch me sadly.
This is the way you want me—
asleep, quiescent, almost dead,
sedated by lush immigrant dreams
of global bliss, connubial harmony.

Yet, I shall always remember
and deign to forgive
(long before I am satiated,
long before I am spent)
that last pressured cry,
"your little death."
Under the halcyon light
you would smoke and contemplate
the sea and debris,
that barbaric keening
of what it means to be free.
As if we were ever free,
as if ever we could be.
Said the judge,
"Congratulations,
on this day, fifteen of November, 1967,
Marilyn Mei Ling Chin,
application # z-z-z-z-z,
you are an American citizen,
naturalized in the name of God

the father, God the son and the Holy Ghost."
Time assuages, and even
the Yellow River becomes clean . . .

Meanwhile we forget
the power of exclusion
what you are walling in or out—
and to whom you must give offence.
The hungry, the slovenly, the convicts
need not apply.
The syphilitic, the consumptive
may not moor.
The hookwormed and tracomaed
(and the likewise infested).
The gypsies, the sodomists, the mentally infirm.
The pagans, the heathens, the non-
denominational—
The coloreds, the mixed-races and the reds.
The communists, the usurous,
the mutants, the Hibakushas, the hags . . .

Oh, connoisseurs of gastronomy and *keemun* tea!
My foes, my loves,
how eloquent your discrimination,
how precise your poetry.
Last night, in our large, rotund bed,
we witnessed the fall. *Ours*
was an "aerial war." Bombs
glittering in the twilight sky
against the Star-Spangled Banner.
Dunes and dunes of sand,
fields and fields of rice.
A thousand charred oil wells,
the firebrands of night.
Ecstasy made us tired.

Sir, Master, Dominatrix,
Fall was a glorious season for the hegemonists.

We took long melancholy strolls on the beach,
digressed on art and politics
in a quaint warfside café in La Jolla.
The storm grazed our bare arms gently . . .
History has never failed us.
Why save Babylonia or Cathay,
when we can always have Paris?
Darling, if we are to remember at all,
Let us remember it well—
We were fierce, yet tender,
fierce and tender.

Notes:

Second stanza: "Jing Pingmei"—Chinese erotic novel.

Sixth stanza: Exclusion—refers to various "exclusion acts" or anti-Chinese legislation that attempted to halt the flow of Chinese immigrants to the U.S.

Sixth stanza: Hookworm and tracoma—two diseases that kept many Chinese detained and quarantined at Angel Island.

Sixth stanza: Hibakushas—scarred survivors of the atom bomb and their deformed descendants.

Notes on the Fifteenth Anniversary Edition
of *The Phoenix Gone, The Terrace Empty*

Marilyn Chin

Fifteen years ago, when Milkweed Editions first published *The Phoenix Gone, The Terrace Empty,* I was in my thirties. I had previously published one book, *Dwarf Bamboo.* I had moved, reluctantly, from my beloved San Francisco to San Diego and my first tenure-track job. I had left one bad long-term relationship and was about to venture into another bad long-term relationship. My mother was ill. She and my grandmother would die shortly after the publication of *Phoenix.*

I was armed for a writing career through years of intense study. As an undergraduate I surveyed ancient Chinese poetry under the tutelage of Professors Cheng and Cohen of UMass Amherst. There followed graduate study at the Iowa Writers' Workshop, where I honed my craft with master poets Don Justice and Jane Cooper and worked at translation with Danny Weissbort, Hualing Nieh, and Peter Jay. Later, as a Stegner Fellow at Stanford, I was challenged by Denise Levertov with astute political questions.

Meanwhile, in the Bay Area, the powerful presences of June Jordan, Adrienne Rich, and Maxine Hong Kingston reigned. Meeting these big-sister mentors, while also coming under the sway of such voices as Nellie Wong's, Mitsuye Yamada's, Bell Hooks's, Gloria Anzaldua's, and Cherrie Moraga's, I was radicalized at the grassroots level and was excited by the women-of-color literary movement. These muses confirmed in me the belief that poetry can be an agent for social change.

The era's transformations of awareness informed and influenced *The Phoenix Gone, The Terrace Empty.* The late 1980s and early 1990s was a period of openness and experiment in American letters. Publishers did not fear to take risks with new and emerging voices, and writers of color gave genuine, challenging, and surprising expression to diverse experiences. Emerging from an era that treated diversity as a historical footnote and academic obligation, we recognized that readers hungered for perspectives beyond the obvious and familiar. *Phoenix* was the vehicle for my new insights and ambitions. I sought a fresh literary agenda, both esthetically and thematically.

I entered *Phoenix* conscious of the contradictory passions of my Chinese-American heritage. The Chinese call the unity of opposites yin and yang. In *Phoenix*'s poems, I meditated on the complementary aspects that run through the universe. These poems explore East and West, personal and political, immigrant and transnational identity, history and modernity—and more. I found myself drawn to the push and pull of Buddhist parables and Christian iconography, Zen quiet and Kali rage, formal verse and free variation, Beijing's Tienanmen throes and San Francisco's Angel Island legacy, and withal, personal exultation triumphant over despair.

I wanted to draw on all my classical Chinese training and reclaim Chinese poetry from my modernist predecessors. I spent long nights trying to create a Chinese/English fusion lyric . . . recalling the *jueju, chu,* and *fu* of classical Chinese poetry, while honing a contemporary American idiom. I wanted to reclaim "Chinese-ness" from Pound and Rexroth and simultaneously assert the "anti-Orientalism" of Said, two seemingly impossible terrains. I hoped to achieve the necessary balance and intertextual parody to generate a forum for deeper engagement. I believe that my best work figures assimilation of contradictory aspects of history and self, wherein the passionate songs protesting the Tienanmen massacre and the anti-Chinese racism of America's gold-rush past collude with personal and familial tales to create a memorable immigrant personality.

Eager to embrace what was referred to as "minority discourse," I felt part of a vibrant generation. We rolled up our sleeves in coalition politics, unafraid of such labels as "Asian American," "feminist," or "post colonialist." I considered myself the quintessential activist poet, gladly tackling "identity" and "gender" politics: I determined to confront such issues head-on in my writing. With *The Phoenix Gone, The Terrace Empty,* I proudly offered metaphorical salutes and full-throated anthems.

Of course, the world has changed greatly in the fifteen years since *Phoenix*'s first publication. Now, there seems to be a backlash against "identity poetry." With the election of our new

African-American president some would have us espouse color-blindness, proclaiming that we have passed over into a postracial, postfeminist, postidentity era. I don't believe for a moment that all is hunky dory in America. Now, no less than in the past, we need stubborn, fearless artists who see through hypocrisy and write about the real issues of our existence.

I have not been "rehabilitated" in middle-age. In fact, I want to assure my friends that I am as feisty as ever. I am still very much an activist poet who believes in my lifework: to infuse my art with three powers; to inspire, to illuminate, and to liberate.

I've been pleased and honored to know that *Phoenix* made an impact in its time and continues to make a difference to readers. I thank my loyal readers for keeping the firebird alive. The tributes are too numerous to list. I remember a young woman from San Jose, inspired by "The Floral Apron," who sewed a lovely red appliqué apron for me that arrived special delivery, just in time for Chinese New Year. I remember a young man from New Orleans who brought me a cup of "turtle soup" after my reading as an ironic homage. Many who wrote to me had read "Summer Love" in the *Norton Introduction to Literature.* One student, certain that I was the bad cook in the vignette, queried, "Why did you scramble oysters with eggs? That's not a romantic breakfast!" I will never forget a girl with long red braids at the Dodge Poetry Festival who cried out, "Read 'How I Got That Name' again!" while raising her fist in sisterhood. I'm grateful to Asian-American poets such as Roger Pao and esteemed scholars such as Rahan Ramazani who, in the blogosphere, extolled and defended "How I Got That Name," helping to make it one of the most anthologized poems in contemporary poetry.

Nor can I forget the reader who brought her dog-eared volume of *Phoenix* for me to sign. She said that there are so many greatest hits in *Phoenix* that she returns to it over and over and never tires of it. She likened the book to the Beatles's *White Album.* That was the best compliment of all. Indeed, I had put *Phoenix* together with the utmost care.

As I reread *Phoenix* today, I am proud and amazed at the range of formal and thematic expression. I had striven for a controlled but flexible free-verse of variegated line-lengths, shapes, and lyric categories, for "beautiful" surfaces with "tantalizing imagery" and "sophisticated crafting." Having met with some degree of success, I muse, "Who wrote these poems, that cocky Marilyn Mei Ling Chin?"

The book was a patient ten-year project. I remember some five years of mulling over the exact phrasing of the long title poem, attending to each breath suspension to mimic the thoughts and footsteps of an ancient courtesan—and another five to wrap up the outrageous, sexy allegorical conceit of "Portrait of the Self as Nation." I recall months conjuring up the invisible Cantonese cacophonic cymbals to foreground the heavy beats of "Barbarian Suite." It took hundreds of typewritten drafts (I diligently revised over and over on my manual typewriter) to obtain the lyric compression of "Tienanmen, the Aftermath" intended to meld love and protest in one controlled package. There is the quiet precision of "Clear White Stream" and the various mock, cheeky Chinese lyrics that dare to query, "Is bondage, therefore, a kind of freedom?" Honoring both sides of my literary heritage, the volume offers polyphonic fun and esthetic hybridity, while mindful of Bai Juyi's populist dictum that a good poem must not be overtly academic or self-indulgent and must be understood by one's cousin (he actually said "maid") on a visceral, human level.

Over the years many have asked about the strange, long title. "The phoenix gone, the terrace empty" is an enigmatic line that I borrowed from a poem by Li Bai. The legendary Chinese bird "phoenix" (always a she) is the symbol of the Empress and is both complementary and oppositional to the dragon, symbol of the divine emperor. In folklore, the phoenix/bride is inextricably conjoined with the dragon/groom for all eternity. I chose this title because a woman's story is at the center of this book, engaging female consciousness, female juices, and female sensibility. Throughout these poems the phoenix, the she-bird, is always dressed in full glamorous regalia. In Western conceptions, the creature called "phoenix" is endowed with the ability to survive battle wounds and reemerge unscathed, rising from the ashes of destruction. Albeit the word "immortal" makes any postmodern poet squirm, it is a victorious, immortal bird.

For any poet to explain her art is perilous—and to pontificate on the successes and failures in her literary career is even worse; nevertheless, I am happy to offer these few observations on the fifteenth anniversary of *The Phoenix Gone, The Terrace Empty*. I am grateful to Milkweed Editions for reissuing this volume. After a poet gives birth to a book of poems, she must let her creation go. How the poems will be received, how they might be loved and cherished—or despised, ridiculed, and, worst of all, ignored—is out of the poet's control. Only a foolish poet would believe that she has power over her creation's destiny.

What is fashionable or unfashionable in the transient poetry scene is of no consequence. Ultimately, our convictions will keep our poems strong. Convictions, after all, are timeless underlying values. Convictions cannot be faked, theorized to ash, or merely filigreed over. The longevity of these poems stands as testament to their "authentic" passion and, I believe, to the sympathetic passions of succeeding generations of readers.

ABOUT THE AUTHOR

Photo by Niki Berg

MARILYN CHIN is the author of three books of poetry: *Rhapsody in Plain Yellow, Dwarf Bamboo,* and *The Phoenix Gone, The Terrace Empty,* and the novel *Revenge of the Mooncake Vixen.* She was born in Hong Kong and raised in Portland, Oregon. Her books have become Asian-American classics and are taught in classrooms internationally. She has won numerous awards for her poetry, including the United Artist Foundation Fellowship, the Radcliffe Institute Fellowship at Harvard, the Rockefeller Foundation Fellowship at Bellagio, two National Endowment for the Arts grants, the Stegner Fellowship, the PEN/Josephine Miles Award, four Pushcart Prizes, a Fulbright Fellowship to Taiwan, residencies at Yaddo, the MacDowell Colony, the Lannan Foundation, the Djerassi Foundation and others. She is featured in a variety of anthologies, including *The Norton Anthology of Literature by Women, The Norton Anthology of Modern and Contemporary Poetry, The Norton Introduction to Poetry, The Oxford Anthology of Modern American Poetry, Unsettling America, The Open Boat,* and *The Best American Poetry of 1996.* Featured in Bill Moyers's PBS series *The Language of Life,* she has read and taught workshops all over the world. Recently, she taught at the Iowa Writers' Workshop and was a guest poet at universities in Beijing, Singapore, Hong Kong, Manchester, Sydney, and Berlin. In addition to writing poetry and tales, she has translated poems by the modern Chinese poet Ai Qing and cotranslated poems by the Japanese poet Gozo Yoshimasu. She teaches in the MFA program at San Diego State University.

MORE POETRY FROM
MILKWEED EDITIONS

To order books or for more information, contact Milkweed at
(800) 520-6455
or visit our Web site (www.milkweed.org).

Rooms and Their Airs
Jody Gladding

Reading Novalis in Montana
Melissa Kwasny

Hallelujah Blackout
Alex Lemon

Music for Landing Planes By
Éireann Lorsung

The Book of Props
Wayne Miller

MILKWEED EDITIONS

Founded in 1979, Milkweed Editions is one of the largest independent, nonprofit literary publishers in the United States. Milkweed publishes with the intention of making a humane impact on society, in the belief that good writing can transform the human heart and spirit.

JOIN US

Milkweed depends on the generosity of foundations and individuals like you, in addition to the sales of its books. In an increasingly consolidated and bottom-line-driven publishing world, your support allows us to select and publish books on the basis of their literary quality and the depth of their message. Please visit our Web site (www.milkweed.org) or contact us at (800) 520-6455 to learn more about our donor program.

Milkweed Editions, a nonprofit publisher, gratefully acknowledges sustaining support from Anonymous; Emilie and Henry Buchwald; the Patrick and Aimee Butler Family Foundation; the Dougherty Family Foundation; the Ecolab Foundation; the General Mills Foundation; the Claire Giannini Fund; John and Joanne Gordon; William and Jeanne Grandy; the Jerome Foundation; Constance and Daniel Kunin; the Lerner Foundation; Sanders and Tasha Marvin; the McKnight Foundation; Mid-Continent Engineering; the Minnesota State Arts Board, through an appropriation by the Minnesota State Legislature, a grant from the Wells Fargo Foundation Minnesota, and a grant from the National Endowment for the Arts; Kelly Morrison and John Willoughby; the National Endowment for the Arts; the Navarre Corporation; Ann and Doug Ness; Ellen Sturgis; the Target Foundation; the James R. Thorpe Foundation; the Travelers Foundation; Moira and John Turner; Joanne and Phil Von Blon; Kathleen and Bill Wanner; and the W. M. Foundation.

MINNESOTA
STATE ARTS BOARD

NATIONAL
ENDOWMENT
FOR THE ARTS
A great nation
deserves great art.

TARGET.

THE McKNIGHT FOUNDATION

Designed by Don Leeper
Typeset in Calisto
by BookMobile Design and Publishing Services

CPSIA information can be obtained
at www.ICGtesting.com
Printed in the USA
JSHW021255170922
30488JS00001B/4

9 781571 314390